CROCUS

FIVE WOMEN

Poetry by women

GOREU ARF. ARF DYSG

STANWELL SCHOOL

This Prize was presented to

Shelley Moon-Brewer

for Academic Achievement

Malcolm Parker

Head Teacher

Date 6/4/'95

CROCUS

FIVE WOMEN POETS

First published in 1993 by Crocus

Crocus books are published by Commonword Ltd, Cheetwood House, 21
Newton Street, Manchester M1 1FZ.

Commonword gratefully acknowledges financial assistance from the
Association of Greater Manchester Authorities, Manchester City Council
and North West Arts Board.
Commonword also wishes to thank Marks & Spencer and Business in the
Arts for their invaluable support.

Crocus books are distributed by Password (Books) Ltd, 23 New Mount
Street, Manchester M4 4DE

Cover illustration by Brent Linley. Cover design by Hemisphere, 47
Newton Street, Manchester M1 1FT
Produced by Commonword and Caxton's Final Film, 16 Nicholas Street,
Manchester M1 4EJ.
Printed by Shanleys, 16 Belvoir Street, Tonge Fold, Bolton.

British Library Cataloguing-in-Publication Data. A catalogue record for
this book is available from the British Library.

Contents

Introduction   ix

Pat Winslow
It Sounds Like Autumn   3
Humming Bird   4
When Juries Burn the Truth   7
The Women Wash   8
Like it's Summer Again   10
Little Britain   11
For Fun   12
Ivory   13
Coffee Morning   14
Mushroom Magic   15
Barry Manilow   17
Sheets Billowing on the First Day of Winter   18
The In and Out cafe, Todd Street   19
Widowed   21
A Silent Fall   23
White Boys   24
Two Moons - September 16th 1992   25

Barbara Bentley
Young Madonna   29
Cracked   30
Removal   31
Division   32
Still Life   33
Blackberrying with Daniel   34
Eye Test   35
Song of the Woman Past Forty   36
Stroke   37
Uncle Nat   38
Stone Cold   39

Chin Wag   40
Excalibur   42
Real Writing   43
Susan's Evening   44

Marguerite Gazeley
Conference   49
A Fire of Words   50
Housewives' Choice   51
Next Stop Bamako   52
Poet   53
The Apex   54
Images   56
Columbus Day   57
First Love   59
Sappho   61
Ancestors   63
Kemi   65
Stiff Upper Lip   67

Sheila Parry
Birthright   71
Hostage   73
Last Rites   74
Full Circle   76
Young Love   77
Easter Flowers   78
The Literary Circus   79
Untouchables (Roumania)   81
The Lines are Down (To D.C.)   82
Summer Wedding   83
Table Talk   85
Return Visit   86
Exchanging Gifts   87

Frances Nagle

Leaving the Artist 91
Steeplechase Park 92
Purveyors 93
Something Aunt Rosie Said 94
Looking for Heathcliff 96
Bala 98
Epithalamion 98
Lips 99
Filial 100
Strangers Passing 101
Visit to the Illuminator 102
'Modern Times' at Manchester
   City Art Gallery 103

Biographies 109

Introduction

When Commonword asked for submissions for a collection of contemporary women's poetry we were unprepared for the quantity and quality of work submitted. Over 100 women from the North West submitted up to 20 poems each which led to much Christmas reading for the editing panel!

The five women finally selected all express hope and optimism about their own and others' lives. Each of the five has developed a strong sense of their own voice, using their subject matter with assurance.

In 'Hostage', Sheila Parry takes an historical moment and creates a powerful image of freedom with which we can identify.

Barbara Bentley, in 'Blackberrying with Daniel', shares the gentle delights of spending an afternoon with a young child, evoking our own childhood memories.

In a light and mischievous vein Marguerite Gazeley's 'Apex' offers a chance meeting and shared confidences in a chainstore changing room. Read it to your friends!

'Filial' by Frances Nagle has resonances for us all. She captures a tender and compelling moment between a mother and daughter that remains long after the reading.

In 'Humming Bird' we learn much of the passion and intimacy of an enduring love. Pat Winslow has crafted a moving celebration.

Together these women offer a clarity of vision which is both inspiring and provocative.

We would like to thank our editors, Cheryl Martin and Louise Rainbow, for their invaluable support.

Freya Rodger
Commonword

Pat Winslow

It Sounds Like Autumn

It sounds like autumn
the pain of leaves
turning grass turning
over in their morning
sleep waking later
than they did
the day before.
It sounds like autumn
crispness hissing
in the dew
the birdsong gone
fragile overnight.
My room is filled
with cold still air
and yesterday's plumpness
has turned to bone again
as I sit staring
at the hard floor
the purple floor
carpet the colour
of burnt heather.

Humming Bird

The messages encoded
on my skin
in my skin

the memories of the last
twenty four
hours we shared

fingertip light and palms pressed
together
like flowers

the roll over in the dark
hug cuddle
kiss sweet brush

of lips wet humming bird night
beating blood
in my veins

dipping drinking and climbing
the final
flight so high

and sudden. The wind was in
our faces
yesterday

trees whispered wave upon wave
on the hill
red mushrooms

secret toadstools folded in
earth and grass
and dark leaves

were menstrual pearls rising
to meet your
enquiring

fingers   brown fungi cupped rain
in the damp
green shadows

and mud sucked against our boots
side by side
stride by stride

the length of our legs measured
the distance
from our home

side by side our palms pressed close
and closer
still again.

Today as I shop stand queue
lock my bike
to railings

and lamp posts go to the bank
wait my turn
for a neat

barber's haircut I feel those
moments like
small feathers

against my skin. Tomorrow
I shall feel
this day's night's

events   your return from work
our evening
meal your smile

as you sit down next to me
your jumper
soft scratching

my face into millions
of starburst
explosions

I shall remember these things
our lips thighs
tongues palms cheeks

touching the rough smooth of the
carpet's pull
your warm voice

in my ear. I shall feel all
this like new
waves breaking

upon an old shore and I
shall love you
even more.

When Juries Burn the Truth

The guilty hide
behind closed doors
they turn their TVs on
and wipe their faces clean
of sweat and fear.

But flickering pictures
tell no lies
and flickering flames
won't provide a smokescreen.
The whole world sees

when juries burn the truth.

The Women Wash

The women wash.
The women wash and wring.
They bend and stoop
and straighten shirts
out on the lines

whilst khaki kings
take photographs of them
for souvenirs.
Begetters
and blood letters.

The dog-tagged gods
spawn tiny living limbs
with hand grenades
held close between
their conquering legs.

The women wash
and wring and another
generation
rises lost -
the kind of dust

that blows between
two nations and settles
in barbed wire camps
with just a name
connecting them.

My father's land.
The land of deserters.
And the women
are hanging
their anger out

for all to see
for the daily papers
to photograph.
For the record.
Not for souvenirs.

Like it's Summer Again

I want soft to release me

not quick
not strange
not sudden

I want the unexpected

gentle
guessed at
hinted at

the warm safe touch of slow hands

a hard
shoulder
pressing close

I want strong to release me

and wide
and full
and open

honest wet mouths lip to lip

your smile
to wake
me make me

feel like it's summer again.

Little Britain

So here we are in the piss and grime
of the nineteen nineties.
The I own you own mentality
that swaggers down our high streets
and stalks our neighbourhoods
with its watch schemes and car alarms.

Where perfect squares of grass are minded
by fuck-off conifers.
Where a daisy equals disorder.
There's nothing flowering here.
They only let lines in.
Straight white ones, of course. Their own kind.

For Fun

Blue red grey green navy white yellow brown
mustard turquoise purple black
twist and flap twist and flap
peg peg peg peg peg peg peg
prop.
This poem has lines of washing in it.

Ivory

Carved out of itself
chiselled into its own likeness
its sheer bulk and weight

has been reduced to
more acceptable proportions
something which can now

be controlled   picked up
taken down   examined   dusted
and shown around   then

put back in place.
Killed only to be born again
as some souvenir

it is destined to
stand in silence forever on
someone's mantelpiece.

A polished trophy.
A smoothed down tragedy. Whitewashed.
And the blood soaked field

of its birth dries in
hexagons. The African plain
is losing them all.

Coffee Morning

We talked by pale November light
sipping coffee from mugs that were
as small and compact as she was
and as her eyes lit up each corner of the room
a gentle peace touched upon my shadow-self
like a slim shaft of sunlight
catching dancing motes unawares.
The clock ticked away the hour
and a cat sat watching us from the cold outside
its face a blur in the mottled window.
We were amused by its direct gaze
and I recalling my cat
ripe pod of pregnancy
stretched out by the fire at home
left then saying I would call again -
comfort in the hands and smiles of friends
too fragile to cling on to for so long.
A nervous grasp like mine could break it.

Mushroom Magic

The old woman gathers
words like morning mushrooms.
She waits all night for them
watching their cool bare heads
pushing up through the leaves.

She pinches them between
her thumb and forefinger
snaps their fat white flesh
out of the loamy soil.
She is their mother now.

She will store them safely
in low wooden boxes
where the shed's slatted light
slants across the dust motes.
She will count them daily

and brush the pale cobwebs
off their damp smelling skins.
Then she will take them out
when she needs to. When she
wants them for weaving spells.

Now she is opening
her pockets wide like mouths
and dropping each one in
like a firm ripe promise.
She is walking with them

cradled against her palms.
And as the morning's dew
begins to lift she rolls
them over and over
in her mind sucking on

each of their names: frugal
lamplight tabernacle
loft pebble spatter toast
creak sellotape amber
Leamington Spa. She laughs.

The old woman throws back
her head and roars out her
delight. Leamington Spa
will do very nicely today
she thinks. After breakfast.

Barry Manilow

They are sedately sitting
these ladies with the silver tea spoons.
Delicately sniffing

into blue paper tissues
they wipe their noses from side to side
as lightly as they would

break off a piece of scone and
place it in their waiting 'o' shaped mouths.
Their nails are perfect pink

like the pearly lipstick marks
that they leave imprinted on the pale
blue china of their cups.

Above the chink and tinkle
of their laughter - over their lowered
voices - a record plays.

In Russell's darkened tea rooms
Barry Manilow is singing to
Bolton's white middle class.

Sheets Billowing on the First Day of Winter

The thin shadow fattens across the ground
then narrows to a strip again
playing games amongst the thawed out dog turds
playing games with the shattered bricks
it darts in and out
like a broken wave
vainly searching for something dry to crash against -
Then silence as the wind abates
and ice cream colours ripple in the sun.
There is a distant hum
of something washing down below
there is the drum of clothes being turned.
In a moment we will have flags everywhere.
There will be a carnival in my yard.

The In and Out cafe,
Todd Street

Chipped china mugs
the radio on
fried egg sandwiches
dripping gold
down old men's chins
each person is
an island in this
steamed up sea
of warmth and noise.
No one bothers
to take their jacket
off 'no one
likes to stay that
long. They're only
here for the chat you
see   they're here
to fill themselves
with a sense of
camaraderie
before going
home to their lives.
Bedsit rooms and
widower's flats   flat
caps on the
pegs where damp brown
overcoats hang down
from the backs of doors.
There too are
spoons puddling up
the tables with
their tea spills   there too

the odour
of yesterday's
fat gone cold in
the pan. But a flick
of the switch
and there is a
cheerful blaze from
the radio   an
instant friend.
Twin barred fires may
hum dismally
in the grey of an
afternoon
but with music
playing and once
or twice some news some
view of what
is happening
they can feel a
part of this world. Just
sometimes they
have a need for
something warm in
their lives   something that
reminds them
of what people
really sound like
and so they come here
and I watch them.

Widowed

His white plastic goggles
hang in the hallway
not his coat nor his cap
nor his thick green scarf.

Down the grey road and up
over the next hill
just a short journey
taken before six

the furnaces blast
and spark   smoke inking
the flat colourless sky
where seagulls drift like

forgotten torn up rags.
She pours hot water
on tea   swills the dark leaves
round and stares outside.

The orange men   the town's
hammer heart beat   are
already working their
muscles forged like steel.

She has removed all that
was soft about him
the things that smelt of pipe
tobacco. Only

his goggles and his watch
remain. Sometimes though
she remembers the blue
industrial scars

that pitted his pale hands
and face   the morning cough
that always came to her
like a cold knife plunge.

She draws the curtain then
and surrounds herself
with night as if the white
day would shrivel her

to nothingness burn her
to ashes   then she
dusts and wipes and cleans until
the foundry hooter blows.

A Silent Fall

A hammer bangs distantly
in the stillness of a limp white afternoon
and leaves fall like forgotten reminders
an event that took place years ago.
Equally distant are the fragments
of a dream I had this morning
soft white flesh beneath my lips and tongue
and the unexpected hardness of nipples
resting pebble-like in the palms of my hands.
When I awoke I was restless
and I've been filling myself up ever since.
First it was toast, then tea, then egg
and now a second meal with the third one
already prepared.
There are leaves too, inside of me
they are falling all the time.
Soon I will have to light the fire
and fill the house with brightness.
Soon I will have to pretend
that all this never happened.

White Boys

In the minute's silence an engine ticked.
We bowed our heads as we held the traffic up.
A banner flicked in the air like washing
then fell limp. A man bent low and stroked a dog.
Someone coughed. Blood on the streets again. Black blood.

The right on white boys with the roaring mouths
were still for once   their papers hugged to their chests.
Leather jackets creaking impatiently
they checked their watches - empty vessels anxious
to fill the streets - then they resumed their chanting.

As we moved off past the doorways of shops
and restaurants they called for unity.
Blood on the streets. Not their blood. Not white blood.
But still they called for it believing in their
supremacy. Their voices were fists and knives.

Two Moons -
September 16th 1992

There are two moons.
One that looks like
a fistful of snow
and one that is as crisp
as hospital sheets.
A pane of glass
makes all the difference.

Last night I sat
in my garden
and watched the thick cold
breath of a plane slicing
across it - a sigh
in white - and thought
of the silver drip

feeding into
your left arm
a foreign body
of long names suspended
in clear cool liquid
as innocent
looking as water.

I remembered
how the plastic
wrinkled as the drips
ticked away like minutes
remembered your face
as you agreed
to this invasion.

A ball of ice
clenched in me then
and didn't loosen
its grip until later
when everyone
had gone to bed.
Alone on the bench

I saw it all:
two moons   the first
hard frosts   dark grey pods
rattling in the wind.
And new leaves. I saw
next year's branches
already growing.

Barbara Bentley

Young Madonna

One day after the birth and you are so slim.
Only your cheeks belly with contentment.
Your hospital bed, decked in cellophane bows,
is about to sail in some regatta.

And you are so confident with flesh.
When you lower baby in the slippery water
you handle the spasms of his jerking limbs
as adroitly as a great performer.

Now infant is at your breast.
Your newly permed hair spirals down.
The anglepoise lamp floods your face
as you and he are icon.

I envy your assurance.
This new life screaming in my arms
has made me jittery: an amateur
awed by the throb of those fontanelles.

Cracked

It was always a ghastly bathroom -
harsh blue and gilt-trimmed.

'We'll get round to it someday,' we said.
Our nest demanded more urgent repairs.

'But in the meantime, we'll mend
that cracked tile,' so we said.

Oh, too safe. Too busy.
Too busy for cracked tiles.

The crack deepens. Half the tile is gone.
There is grey mouldering plaster beneath.

But we cracked a bottle each weekend,
staring through each other's crazed face.

Oh, but I loathe this shriek of blue,
this leering blue, with its fissured tile.

I kick with the force of the pelting shower.
Out, out, damned crack.

The remnant falls. Ceramic flour settles
to grey powder on cold vinyl.

Removal

A cloud-torn sky. This garden
was reclaimed from such wilderness.
Hedgerows stormed my hands.
Black clods, stubborn in drizzle,
stayed spade-struck.

After the taming, a merry summer
when colours jostled for supremacy.
Then huge winter. A lycra sky
stretched over the white lawn.
Big moon gazed like a voyeur.

This spring, in light thin as skimmed milk,
I take my leave, garden.
The tea chests are packed; our lives
wrapped and stacked and awaiting removal.
The bulbs we planted are buried deep.

Division

'We are separated'
I hear myself say to well-meaning people.
As if we were curd and whey
or some referee had parted us two
wrestlers sparring in the ring of life.
As if we were milk and cream
or some great ocean, forged by God's wrathful hand,
instantly divided us, for Eternity.

'We are separated'
I say, and well-meaning people reply
'Oh, I'm sorry, I didn't know.'
Perhaps this news should be scooped on the front page,
or levered in a coffin, and sent ceremoniously
to the graveyard of wrecked marriages
where the taboo of grief can fester.

'We are two'
I want to say, head held high.
We were never
    Two hearts beating as one
    Two souls united in Heaven's match
    Two halves made whole.
Never that, I can say, with no bitterness.
We sparked together, but smouldered intact.
Our children are the blood link.
That is all.

Still Life

This cove is sanctuary where she makes restitution
warming her hands in sand infused with blood warmth.
Children at the shoreline are dwarfed
by a wide sky that seeps in the sea.

Suppose that, from the smudge,
horses rear up, massive as legends,
their eyes aghast, their manes flung tempests,
their riders judgmental as scythes -

instead of those birds scrawled on grey:
children's Vs at the corner of a page
which she crumples up, not hearing them -
those hooves that tread water in stiller depths.

Blackberrying with Daniel

Sun glints on leaves like green pennies.
Blackberries hang dark and luscious,
unreservedly yielding.

Their juices spill over my hands
like ink. Autumn promise
is in their purpling dusks.

You urge me deeper into the bush
where sunlight hardly penetrates
filmy webs and darkened barbs.

Scudding August clouds
are netted in the dark tangle
as my arms reach deeper

to touch the just ripe yield
hanging as tantalisingly
as baubles on a children's tree.

I lean forward; balance to grasp
lobes quivering on that twig.
These I must have: perfections.

You proffer your basket full of indigo
when I pluck them. My arms are scarred.
The deep dyes trickle over wicker.

Tomorrow the rolled pastry will lid
blackberries spiced with cinammon.
We shall savour August before nights draw in.

Eye Test

When he looms before her,
the pin light of his torch
pricking her pupils, she can see
his strafed skin, so cratered
because he is less than an eyelash away;
there is a glisten that could be orange zest.
She can see his nostrils, at this range
dark and filamented, and feel his breath
warming her cheek like a soft touch.

She wonders how she must seem to him -
whether her blemishes are magnified,
or whether his professional stance
has made him myopic or blind.

But this transaction
is a tacit agreement
that the two parties
decline the invitation
implied in an intimacy
often denied lovers.

So they shun spectacle,
and she clearly sees
that we are best seen at some distance
and the brailles of contact are kisses
sealed with closed eyes.

Song of the Woman Past Forty

Just rough me a scourging exfoliating scrub.
Rigour me a vigorous cellulite rub.
Tone me. Cleanse me. May the tingle of astringent
dewy-freshen cheeks till they glow refulgent.
With whipped creme anoint me.
With face mask appoint me
born again woman, resculptured, resplendent.

Oh let me not lapse into a Brooknered malaise,
but sing me a song of japonica'd days
Dior me. Lauder me. May rejuvenating scents
burn holes in my purse and my too common sense.
Let liposomes unwrinkle me
and neosomes retwinkle me -
I, who was ravaged by my cold-cream innocence.

And give me the gall to dye my greying roots
or waste all my wage in a blow-out at Boots.
'Try me', 'Test me', woo concoctions I select
from the alchemists' trove that defies intellect.
May wild claims come true
and the phoenix rise new
from the ashes of fictions - the words that have wrecked.

Stroke

It's a pampering of fingers on skin, so at that critical moment
life is no more enticing than a Monday morning clock.

Not this. A thug bashed you against the ropes.
At the last count you got up, still ticking.

Ticking now. That click in your throat.
You cannot name those peas which you shell.
Those peas which you shell, willing
that rhythm of fingers you use for shelling.
But the fingers are shocked into stiffness;
the peas so arthritic they will not yield in your hands.

To stroke your flecked hands back to stillness.
To hear your breath come as rasps, then soften

as your head nods. A clock stops as quietly
as dusk flapping at the gingham.

Uncle Nat

Tick of your fob watch, tick insistent
wills you to fill those protracted days
drawn in like your Woodbines; the persistent

stubbing out of each habitual phase
is recorded on the barometer,
its needle clocking the appropriate phrase

ranged within the walnut perimeter -
every gradation from rainy to fair -
the aneroid dial a chronometer

of changes stippling the local air.
But the timepiece within you ticks its sweet lies
or is out of step with the time elsewhere.

You smile at the irony of disguise -
of stoop and splutter so we call you old man -
though you know you're a lad, and just as wise

as the boys made erudite at Verdun,
where you also harvested a yield of years
too bruised for salvaging. Returning home

a precocious boy, you were ill at ease
with times cliched jokes: the tacky parade
of leaf to tree, and the winter striptease

since you saw it all. Seed to skeleton
fast-forwarded you to war veteran.

Stone Cold

In the coffin,
image of you as you were.
Sun parodies breath
over your white gown.

Your heart is stopped.
Stopped irreversibly -
an overwound clock.
I cannot make you go again.

Your eyes are trapped
under onyx.
Your fingers, cigarettes -
thin paper and ash.

My skin is needles.
Need I say that I shiver
at the sin of kissing
your corpse that is not

you.

Chin Wag

We had the big wedding at Chalfont Street church.
I promised to love, honour, and obey.

I love after closing time. Come morning
I pack my stranger's snap tin.

I honour with dinner kept warm
between two plates over a pan.

I obey when he calls me 'woman'.
At night I keep my trap shut.

I'm a good wife. I look for gaps
somewhere between these promises.

Around mid-morning there's a chink -
slight, like the hole in the parlour curtains.

With other good wives I can step in that chink
which widens when we've donkeystoned steps

and the street yawns, emptied of menfolk.
Then we exchange words like pennies

or Woodbines. Gossip is barter.
I hoard life in my apron pocket.

'That Lillian, the one at 57, you know,
brassy lass - she's in the family way ...'

But there's jobs to be done. No use standing idle.
Promises press down. The gap narrows.

'That Lillian's a stupid bitch.
She's gone and dug herself a hole.'

Excalibur

An arm, a hand like an axe
reared above the bed. Adrenalin
jolted me. Was this intruder
or nightmare apparition?

But it was neither. The limb
so raised, wielding dark air
in its white-knuckled grip
was my hand, quivering executioner.

Was this the self of dream come to kill?
It was not my recognisable hand -
my woman's hand, made for caring;
my writer's hand, moribund.

From a deep, hushed lake,
my hand rose like a harbinger.
It had done with all its women's work
and grasped its own excalibur.

Real Writing

That pavement edged the terraces
in a line of moss.
We grubbed out crevices and skipped the nicks.
You must beware of cracks.
This we played one summer morning
till we stopped, flabbergasted, in our tracks.

What shocked us were maggots.
They squirmed like cursives
drawn on the mossy guideline
from the witch's house right down the road.
It was joined-up writing after coy print:
a secret message we could not decode.

From doors left ajar
I read the runes of adult whispers -
saw the crone sprawled at the foot of her stairs,
the rancid meat that buzzed with flies
and maggots the colour of contusions
crawling in sockets that were her eyes.

In my Dali fantasy
maggots are dripping watches.
Time betrayed the crone
but conspired to make her fall
from woman to spinster to neighbourhood witch
a revelation in adult scrawl.

Susan's Evening

Swings, newly abandoned,
are still tipsy. A see-saw
recovers stasis.

They have gone. Imprints of soles
clog the roundabout spool
that is still unreeling.

But Susan stays.
She grips the swing chain so hard
rust bloods her palms.

She ponders evening
leaning out like a damp slide.
Anticipation. No surprise.

She will walk back; feign unconcern
on seeing the space where his van is not.
Only dusk is parked there.

The unused swing will swing
and rides subside into night
in other children's dreams.

But Susan waits for dad's voice
gravelling the downstairs rooms
with his own last orders.

Then she will listen for hush -
the house settling; stasis confirmed -
she will print the pillows with rust;

see all her evenings damned by his drink.
They will be
empty parks filled with dusk.

Marguerite Gazeley

Conference

She spoke so quietly
At the conference
All of us outspoken
Thinking that we understood
Because we cared

She spoke so quietly
I wondered if I'd heard
'Excuse me, but your
Ignorance is showing.'

So quiet yet
I felt it like a
Bruise upon the heart
A deep and welling purple.

Blushed and stammered.
While my thoughts flew
Here and there
Like startled sparrows

Later in deep thought
I knew it was
A necessary wound
That would not heal
But always flow

With questions.

A Fire of Words

Just as a frozen limb
will feel no pain
until the warmth
of sun or fire
sends the blood tingling
through the veins

so with the fire of words
that thaws a frozen heart.
The hurt that must be
passed through
will be feared

Should it be sought?
Should hearts melt?
Their pain is slight
compared to that
which lit the fire of words

and keeps it burning

Housewives' Choice

I love to hear your dignified defence of dust
your graceful giving in to grease

let pots and pans await their turn and kettles rust
let strivings for perfection   cease.

For we at home could spend our days reflected
in cold chrome
becoming alien to our warm slow selves, deflected
from the life beyond

Come in and talk, come have a cup of tea
I won't care any more
my home will always be untidy but it keeps
a warm and hopeful welcome   just like me.

Next Stop Bamako

I go there when I'm ironing ...
sizzle of steam
shirt sleeve half smoothed
I am not here ...
I am where the music takes me

Mali ... Casamance ... and Abidjan

So far I have not
burned a hole in
table cloth or sheet
But it's a miracle
because I'm not here

I'm listening to the
tama ... balafon ... and kora

So far I have not
found a miracle
strong enough
to keep my double
working here efficiently

so I can change the
silver wings of thought
for a jet ...

next stop Bamako

Poet

You are the zest of lemons
You are the tang of salt
You are the crunch of cornflakes

You are the yeast that leavens
the bread of plain existence

Your words are challengïng
like chillies, fire like peppers
sting of vinegar and spike of spice

You are sugar when you want to be
never long enough to dull with sweetness

You are bubbles rising
you are the fizz and flavour
in the soda stream of life.

The Apex

He was the apex of our triangle,
this we discovered, in the cluttered angle
of a chainstore changing room,
as I remarked on her perfume:
'Valkyrie?' I ventured. 'Yes, it's awful,
my boyfriend buys it, by the drawerful,
and he insists it smells just fine!'
'Oh yes!' I spluttered, 'so does mine!'

'Mini?' I murmured, for we had both selected
the same blue mini skirt, and both rejected
in similar material, a pair of jeans.
'My boyfriend likes me wearing them
as long as I don't talk to other men,
but they can stare, he thinks that's fine'
'That's funny' I said 'so does mine!'

So side by side, in the stark mirror, we compared
our looks, our shoes, our choice of clothes, our hair,
and realised that both of us had been obedient to the self
same whim and both of us were dressing just for him.

And as we surfaced from delusion,
we came as one to this conclusion,
that she was Monday, Wednesday, Friday,
and I was all the other days except for Sunday!
We looked into each other's eyes
and promised him a big surprise.

On Tuesday next, at half past eight,
unknown to him, a double date.
At Henry's wine bar on the Strand
we sat in state, a pint of shandy in each hand

and as we sat, we savoured it,
spicy sweat of unshaved armpit,
bliss of baggy dungarees
rolled up towards our freckled knees
and just enough designer stubble on our shins.
We both relaxed our double chins
and smiled, real smiles at the assembled company,
and were rewarded with a boyish grin
from weary worldly men drowning the day in gin,
who'd fed their youth to ravenous computers
and now, were last train possible commuters.

So occupied were we, and feeling so alive,
we did not notice him arrive.
We did not catch the shudder on his face,
the ripple of recoil in back and shoulder blades,
as he abruptly left the place.

I looked at her,
She looked at me.
We both dissolved in girlish glee
and drank to his departure long and deep,
and to the friendship we would keep
forever, for we both agreed
that though our choice had proved regrettable,
his taste in girlfriends was impeccable.

Images

I have seen your image
plundered from pyramids,
kept in glass cases,
carved upon stone.

And yet you are here now
Woman of Africa,
sunfire surrounds you,
lit from within.

Aflame like a phoenix,
you rise from the ashes
of grey city streets
and grey city minds.

Columbus Day

What errant wind was blowing, Cristobal?
What tide was restless on the shore of Genoa
the night you were born?

You thought you heard the voice of God
as you embarked on perilous uncharted seas

What curious angel sparked your uncertainty
your absolute belief that you had found Cipangu
distant Ophir and the treasures of the East?

Yet you are feted, celebrated
for your brave and brazen vision

first-footing through the door into
the New World   old familiar ground
to those who watched your ships come in.

Whatever lies within the spirit of discovery
could never justify the wreck of lives
on shores you chanced upon Don Cristobal
Colon   named for a dove

Did you feel the chill wind, eagle clawed
which followed you, bearing the birds of prey?

Does your spirit know the spirits of the dispossessed
who throng my thoughts,
Where are the days for Arawak, Carib and Taino?
Are there enough days in the calendar to honour
all who discovered you suddenly amongst them
uninvited   unashamed

Columbus   weep with me
You cannot change what was   but what will be?

Columbus, sail your ghostly galleon
to the scenes of costly fanfares.
Visit the dreams of those who hail your name

Tell them every trumpet blast dishonours
those who died, man, woman, child
It is the simplest courtesy to be quiet
    and remember ...

First Love

When I was ten, my friend and I
spent hours in the tree house
talking
of when we would be journalists
and writers
holding hands sometimes
exchanging solemn kisses
as the ash leaves swayed
above our heads
One day he said he loved me
I knew that I loved him
all summer long
the world was at our feet
and we were happy
in the branches of our home

One day I read a magazine
telling of wicked teenagers
who held hands in public
kissed each other on street corners
And then a grown-up asked me
what I thought we were up to
my friend and I
spending so much time together
The words did not make sense
but I understood the tone
and I felt we must have sinned
though I did not know how

That afternoon I told him
'I don't love you anymore'
and saw his face turn pale
his hurt eyes search for meaning

I had none   except other people's
He left the room
and closed the door
My heart felt like a fragile bowl
dropped from a great height
the fragments sharp inside my chest
where once had been a smooth place
filled with light
He closed the door forever
separated by a phrase
a garden wall   a lifetime
splinters of that pain remain
and I remember vividly
Does anyone forget?

I hope wherever he may be
that he forgives and understands.

Sappho

Since you mentioned it
I tried to think
when I first heard the word
and I remembered

I didn't hear it
It was in the dictionary
Lesbian, native of the
Isle of Lesbos, I imagined
classical, draped figures
leaning gracefully
upon a column
or rising from a foamy sea
wet-tendrilled hair framing
a dreamy face.

So I was confused a
few years later when I read
Roz is a dirty lesbian
scrawled on the toilet wall

Roz wasn't in my form
being a few years older
She looked very modern
not classical at all
and all her clothes were clean
her shoes shone.
Someone told me lesbians
were girls who hated men
So I asked her one day
if she did, she paused

rolling the word around her
mind as if it were a
term from chemistry or physics
recognised but meaningless

'Men? I don't think of them
as enemies, I don't think
of them at all ... Are you
on first or second dinners?
Sarah says it's chips today!'

Ancestors

My home
my village of the soul
does not exist
no walls, no leaf
enarched for shelter
no roof tree now remains

my ancestors
no map can guide me there
no drums can call me back
but still the embers
of the hearth fire
fires of the heart
refuse to die

This house
holds me prisoner
It has walls within walls
The stones have expectations
but they do not speak
of life
or even of belonging
They disapprove
in a refined
and unrelenting way

It's not my home
but it will be my children's
For them it holds
cradles of memories
They have no other
ghostly imprint
to contend with

Forgive me
Ancestors
that I cannot be
the channel of your
life
to them

Kemi

You are asleep
the dark curve
of your head
above the eiderdown
the pattern of your plaits
upon the lace

grandmother's pillowcase

the picture of
my grandmother
is on the wall
She had beautiful
dark eyes like you

and her expression
elegant and still
can yet suggest
a quiet mischief

I am asleep
and in my dream
you are singing to
my grandmother
in your pure high voice

She would have loved
the way your thoughts
flow like quicksilver
the neat determined angle
of your head

and your eyes
bright like a robin
that comes closest
to the gardener
yet knows it's own ground
to the last defended trill.

Stiff Upper Lip

Goodness me! I wondered where I'd left it!
Wondered why people seemed to stare
as I got off the train   and when I reached the office

Were my stockings torn
my hemline drooping
or even worse
unmentionable bits
of bacon sandwich
clinging to my teeth?

I checked, but still they stared.

'This is the face I was born with!'
I was tempted to yell
'The one that causes total strangers
to clap me on the back and say
'Don't worry darlin', it might never happen!'

Something has happened
something strange
my face feels fit to crack and
I can't seem to stop this   smile
disconcerting all who look my way

They've never seen so many teeth
displayed at once, perhaps
deprived of the usual services
of a genuine made in England
stiff and starchy upper lip

I was attached to it
but now I know
it's found such a good home
I can move on
to the serious business
of having a good time!

Sheila Parry

Birthright

So now we know, sweet sisters,
we possessed the power
long ago;
secret beneath **our** skin,
etched deep in bone
as joy and love
ran singing through our veins,
crackled along nerve ends.

Never equality -
this supremacy,
crowned at the rising of the flesh.
Once it was known
by those who watched
in corners of still rooms
where life met death
and resurrection
sprang out crying,
reaching for the light.

Men always understood
and feared this truth,
dreading a sterile harvest
in the incantations
of a witch.
So they burned us -
set us on fire
with impotent desire,
hollow ambition
echoing in empty arms.

We must retrace our steps,
follow the moon,
swim with the turning tides.
Regain our Queendoms
and the Motherland
that once was ours.

Hostage

The day they brought
the bowl of cherries
to our prison cell
was just like any other day -
one more to live through,
one more to endure,
counting the shades of grey.

We did not eat them
until darkness came,
haunting our room with shadows,
dimming that one bright flame.

We had forgotten red -
only remembered in a careless cut,
the sudden flow
of human blood.
But this was different;
we felt no hunger for the fruit,
no need to taste
or savour sweet, fresh juice.

This was a feast indeed
for starving eyes;
we broke our fast,
the ripe fruit
burst with sweetness
in our mouths
and filled our minds
with memories
of light.

Last Rites

This is the day
we have postponed,
fearing disfavour
from beyond the grave,
your spirit watching
from a corner of the room.

So many clothes
in musty cupboards,
drawers closed tight,
dresses I don't remember,
coats which you forgot;
shoes spilling out from boxes
stacked on dusty shelves.

I make a pile
of crumbling peppermints
and crumpled tissues
plucked from pockets
shaped by knotted hands.

He keeps a handbag
filled with secrets
and the last sad trivia
of your life,
then bids me take your rings;
a diamond promise,
golden vow
and circle of eternity.
The rest I leave -
fake gems which glitter,
winking in the sudden light.
I close the lacquered lid,

returning them to night.

We work as quickly as we can.
He flinches at the pain
of opened wounds,
I hide my guilt
at smooth unbroken skin
until my fumbling fingers
find your mirror
and I bleed,
cut deeply by
a small reflection
of myself.

Full Circle

Her going wasn't planned;
she was the sort
who'd pack for weeks,
write lists,
leave messages.

Instead, she leapt
from one life to the next
and found herself
sleeping on floors,
naked and unashamed.

She left her clothes,
books, jewelry,
and slipped her skin,
emerging raw
and vulnerable.

It took a long time
to accumulate a life,
to grow a shell again.

Now she's cocooned,
surrounded by possessions,
weighted with bric-a-brac.

She shuns deep water,
fears the pull
of tides and currents;
waits and watches,
shivering on the shore.

Young Love

It was the summer time of love,
telling sweet secrets in the singing grass
while daisy-chain gangs
frolicked over fields,
rolled down soft slopes
into a sea of buttercups
drowning in light.

We left our bikes abandoned on the verge,
walked in the woods,
cooled our hot blood
beneath tall trees.

When we returned the questioning began.
Clouds formed to hide our innocence,
we tasted guilt.

Next day it rained,
we stayed indoors - confined
and missed the rainbow
when it split the sky.

Easter Flowers

These lilies do not blow,
they are still,
fixed in their purity
set against stone.

The ordered symmetry of ritual
moves on
and we sit here,
the partly living,
watched by these pale, stiff sentinels of death.

Seeking escape, I look for lilac,
long for its sensuous scent,
remember broken alabaster,
sweet spikenard
and flowing hair
covering His human feet.

The Literary Circus

Roll up! Roll up!
See where they come - the shining ones -
the Literati, Glitterati,
holding court in canvas temples
while the faithful queue to cheer.

Their heads are heavy now
with words and fantasies
but look behind blind eyes
where swinging skeletons and long dry bones
are burning, turning in the mid-day sun.

Here come the posers
and the media crew;
the planners and arrangers,
Arts Council bureaucrats,
riding hobby horses,
juggling with too little cash.

And now the readers enter,
sitting below small gods
in hard seats not reserved
for those who know but do not understand.

Here come the writers
severed from their solitude
to be interrogated, questioned and confused;
dazzled by spotlights,
grilled on burning issues of the day.

Last are the critics,
clowns with painted tears
on fixed white faces.

Tumbling and falling out,
playing with fears.

Only the secret poets,
tightrope artists,
walk a straight and narrow path.
Not wired for sound,
they carve the air like angels,
yet still keep one foot
firmly on the ground.

Untouchables (Roumania)

Here on this crowded bed
I cower,
foetus-curled and small
beside
my twisted sisters.

And we are
dumb to tell
our pain -
paralysed by loss.

Our senses starved
we die
by inches.

Let us alone
and do not touch -
your kindness
is a wound
too terrible to bear -

even for us.

The Lines are Down
(To D.C.)

I can't believe you've gone,
still, after all this time,
I read a poem,
see a play,
hear music that you'd like
and want to phone you,
hear your swift response.

I did that once -
heard shrill ringing
echoing through empty rooms.

Now I know
your number's disconnected,
dead.
My fingers hesitate,
what would I say
if you should answer me?

The gap between us now
is far too wide
for trivial chat;
your traveller's tales
too strange for telephones.

And I'm afraid
that you might call me back.

Summer Wedding

Here, in this quiet place
I sit surrounded
now by stones;
names etched in grief,
guarded by headless angels,
dressed with faded flowers.

Beneath my feet they lie -
beloved husband,
dearest wife -
ashes to ashes,
earth to earth.

The church is locked,
only a fierce sun enters
staining the walls
with saintly glass.

Time here is told by sundial
as the years pass.
This was the path she trod,
wearing brown satin
and a deep-brimmed hat.

I hear her laughter,
see her running
through a sudden shower;
lose her within the shadows
of a sandstone porch.

She kept a photo, blurred,
time-marked by fingers,
and one pink dusty rose

pressed paper thin
as memories of love,
brief as a summer wedding
in the rain.

Table Talk

Her bright talk bubbled
with the soup,
smiles spiced the main course
but dessert was aptly named -
however said,
as silence lay congealed
on greasy plates.

Her going shattered
meal-time grace;
now they speak freely
and in truth
of everything except
that empty place
forever open
like a hungry mouth.

Return Visit

This time I see there's grey dust
on the lamp,
notice an off-white tablecloth.
The waiters seem less gay than camp;
I check inflated prices
on their broken bric-a-brac.

But is it still the same,
this crazy cafe in a narrow street?
Maybe we've changed,
have disobeyed
like Lot's wife looking back.

The sea wind licks our lips
with salt again;
helpless we turn to see
our love dissolving in the rain.

Exchanging Gifts

Your fingers,
skilled with wood,
could fashion furniture;
made me a doll's house once
when toys were scarce,
small casualties of war.
I heard you hammering
each night,
did not appreciate your gifts
of time and craftsmanship.

Your hands,
now twisted, gnarled with age,
will tremble as they pass a cup,
yet you produce
smooth polished bowls,
rounded and begging
to be touched.
Your turning lathe
gives life to ancient apple trees,
you make old, knotted oak
conform to your design.

My way with words
you never valued,
never understood -
until today
I find you trying to write
a tribute to a friend,
now dead.

Taking your speech,
coarse-grained as rough-hewn pine,
I carve and shape,
then plane and polish language,
order your thoughts,
give tongue to love
and fill your empty hands
as you filled mine.

Frances Nagle

Leaving the Artist

I wish I'd never set eyes on you.
I'm trying to gather my things -
My jars, my wicker chair, my canvases;
Trying to get myself together.

You have me hanging everywhere:
All my eyes follow me, unzip
My clothes, and further,
Watch me decompose.

The stone you sent for has arrived.
I shall not stay to see myself
Emerge; to hear my excess
Clink upon the tiles.

I tried to leave you once before.
You often tell it: how you were
Deranged. But I remember
How I sagged back in

And you were urgent, urgent and
Must show me how the sky was brushed
With violet, rose. If you were here
I could not tell you this.

Steeplechase Park

(after a painting by Reginald Marsh)

In Steeplechase Park
We ride and we swing,
We light up in the dark,
We forget all our pain
In the lift and the flight:
Everything's thrilling,
Everything's right.

We roll onto our backs,
Our skirts billow high,
Our legs open slightly,
There's a look in our eye
Alluring the riders
Who smile at us hard
Before they divide us.

In Steeplechase Park
A man tries to mount
The mare of his choice
And finds that he can't.
He wallops her rump,
Then has her shot,
Says the filly won't jump.

Purveyors

'Yes sir. We'll get you any title.
The Joy of Evil. Do you know the author?
Dawn of Darkness. No, we don't deliver.'
Please don't look into my eyes like that sir.

The house is not dissimilar to mine:
Two bedrooms, boxroom, cosy street.
His voice is velvet unction; his pants are tight.
I deliver - night after night after night.

Something Aunt Rosie Said

'Our lads never got a look-in
After the Yanks came.
You were nearly a G.I. baby
In my opinion, but never tell
Your mother I said so.

I remember, night after hot night,
Trying to listen from the window
While they cuddled in our shed,
And did things I couldn't make out
At the time: and some of their names -
Marty, Darren, Wayneford,
B.J. Stevenson the Third.

Our Mam, she said it was
The nylons, instruments of sin,
That those that give them
Think they have the right ...

I was too young for more
Than chewing-gum, but I
Could feel their - I dunno -
Their hugeness, all the space
That each one carried around him,
Colossal magnetic fields, charisma
We'd call it now, pzazz, you'll
Be okay with us babe
The winning team.

Sometimes, afterwards, she'd
Whisper me from her bed
And tell me things.
Oh bliss, she'd say, it's all

Such bliss. I try to think
About them Rosie, out there,
Our boys, and she'd fling her arm out
Showing me the sky; but Rosie, Rosie,
It's all such fun, and Rosie
Darling, you've seen nothing
Till you've seen a Yankee soldier
Loading up his gun.'

Looking for Heathcliff

Today the moor was drenched in cloud,
My gown weighed heavy.
All I could see was wind-scoured
Rock and heather. I searched
For the tracks of his horse,
Felt at the back of caves
For empty wine-skins.

Tonight by the parlour fire
My sister is attentive to the curate,
Who stuffs his smooth pink cheeks
With seed-cake as he chatters.
His fish eyes gleam
But not, I fear, for my sister
Who has told me that she thinks
That she may love him.

On the moor -
He's riding.
The wind that rocks our chimney
Rushes through his hair.
If I draw aside the curtain
I will see how the cloud has lifted;
How under a great white moon
He gallops across the skyline
On his bold black mare -
His body
Close upon her withers
As she beats against the tempest.

Bala

That night the lake went on for ever.
You drove fast and easy, my hand
Between your thighs, my head
Against your shoulder.

So close, that nothing could
Divide us - not a thread
Of moonlight, not the shadow
Of the rabbit who appeared

Before our headlights, flipped
Under our wheels;
To lodge in memory
Its snapped spine and ribs,

And startle me, years later -
The lake road seeming shorter,
I say you drive too fast:
You drive faster.

Epithalamion

Suppose that we unswear our oath;
Untie this knot that binds
Our enemy to us;

Unstitch the white, white dress
From which my body nightly
Soars beside its mortalness;

Untake our photographs;
Unbear our fruit; untwine our stems;
Neuter the oestrus that began

My cursed campaign.
Unbuild the folly that was love
Where no love proved. This done,

Suppose that when we join
In pleasure our capricious flesh,
The enemy is gone.

Lips

They could find no cure;
Though they worked like thin pink worms,
Squeezing out displeasure
And inflexibly right words.

Even kisses that they
Stapled on her didn't heal her
And she grew up still
Yearning to make them smile.

Filial

All day your arms lie at your side like fallen branches.
I search for answers in your fading face.
Was this a goddess, this her mighty fist?
I came as daughters come because they must.
I smooth your hair away maternally.
Where is the juggernaut?
Who is this easy, grateful lady?

I gather you to me.

Strangers Passing:
In memory of my grandparents

They scuttle
To take their places
In the deathtrains.
Taut grey faces.

My videotapes are worn
Thin and pale. Jews
Surge on, but I can
Halt them - Still/Pause:

Check each face.
Not yet. One day they'll pass
And I will know them.
Or will not.

Visit to the Illuminator

The normal eye is out of phase.
So spare the gesture of her nib
We do not see it move, though move
It must, as flowers must unfold.

Our chase is cornered in this room
Where calm is ruling. We begin
To listen for the catch of quill
On vellum; time unwinding.

How can this be so slow?
How can so little happen?
We have driven across centuries
To see a woman doing almost nothing.

Machines can humble every skill
She demonstrates: line; colour;
Pattern; snaking curlicue. 'Why does
She bother?' someone whispers.

She does not answer him with speech.
The hand that hardly stirs
Embellishes beyond his sight
A word.

We move off to another place
Of interest - fast on the heels
Of rumour: truth, inevitably,
Taking longer.

'Modern Times' at Manchester City Art Gallery

'I took away, in sufficient-sized packets, courage to
be an artist, an artist now, amid the gritty crushed
grays of this desperately living city, a bringer of
light and order and color, a singer of existence.'
John Updike

i. Me in Sea

You say - but can I trust you?
I see no water, only life-size woman,
Canvas not quite big enough to hold her,
Bent head gazing straight past her pudenda,
Her skin, her fur, childishly affecting,
Chunky, forthright legs.
Hold on - I'm taking off my dress.

ii. The Silent Ventriloquist

Charlie opens his portcullis of a mouth
To volley abuse at the big dumb man behind him.
No reaction.

'Fight back,' they howl. 'Don't stand for that.'
He ignores it all - invective, kindness.
The audience loves it:

For Charlie Brown's in charge (has been
Since Arthur was a baby crawling across
A battleground of parents) -

'Go on Arthur, tell 'im, tell 'im.
You great girl's blouse,
You tell 'im.'

Not a flicker.
Where Arthur's gone
Nobody can reach him.

iii. Mother and Child

We argue - how much was chance?

How was it on the first day
When the iron-dark stone arrived
Appointed to take part in a conception?
Did he edge round slowly,
Place his palms against the coldness,
Rub his face against it?
Did it surprise him every time
He stopped to breathe; quiver
As he scraped each grain away?
Did she?

You say his vision was complete
Before he touched his chisel;
That he opened up the certain find
After months of calculated digging;
Of danger.
That the woman, when he met her,
When he saw her powerhouse forearm,
Her loadbearing shoulder, the almost
Incidental child heaped on her,
Was no stranger.

iv. Some Like it Hot

Cool title for a man
Who takes a tartan thermos
In his mouth.

In our leaflet
It looks provocative
But holds no threat.

We swan round this fine space
Butt into
Pocked-out skin.

You show me
How the head is hollow,
Eaten thin.

v. On the Edge of the City

On the edge of a city
Down goes down,
The gobful unequivocal.

The painter
With his masterly technique
Spews on success.

His hero steals past
With his bag of tools
(Work or skulduggery)

And books.

vi.

Stepping from the gallery
Into daylight dark,
Hectic in every fibre,
I seek - hoping to catch her
By the arm and warn her -
A woman coming in
Who looks like me.

Biographies

Barbara Bentley
Barbara was born in Bolton but left the North West to study at university in Hull and Birmingham. She returned to teach English at colleges in Wigan and on Merseyside.

Her husband's career took her to London and, subsequently, to the North East where she left work for a time to bring up her children.

Now divorced, she lives with her parents, son and daughter and teaches at Leigh Campus. After work, the children and writing, she has little spare time and considers the extended family a mainstay for single parents.

Barbara was galvanised into writing when a folder of 'a lifetimes' sporadic effort' went missing. A course at Lumb Bank and support from Warrington Writers' Group provided encouragement. She is currently working on short stories and continues to write poetry.

Marguerite Gazeley
I hope these poems speak to you.

Long before I tried to write them, I told stories - travellers' tales. As children can, I felt entirely confident describing places I had never seen, deserts, mountains, seas; and was so fascinated by landscape that the power and mystery of people passed me by. I was nearly seven before I realised that each person holds a world within, a landscape I could not visit by imagining, only by invitation.

So I longed for people to speak to me, to tell me how they saw the world. I loved reading, but listening even more. Hearing poetry in performance for the first time was a great joy; poems by Merle Collins, Grace Nichols, John Agard, Lemn Sissay, Nailah ... which made me think, which called up so many emotions that I still search for words to express them. From a Cultureword poetry evening in 1987, I came to know of the many writing groups within Commonword and Cultureword. I give grateful thanks to all at Womanswrite for their inspiration, challenge and support and to Pauline, Angi, Terry and Christina for unfailing patience, kindness and encouragement.

Frances Nagle
Frances Nagle was born and brought up in Nottingham. She studied Sociology at York University. On graduation she moved to Salford and started a career in teaching. She married 'a man with itchy feet' and they gave up their jobs to travel overland to India and Nepal, spending time en route in Turkey, Iran, Afghanistan and Pakistan.

She now lives in Marple Bridge with her husband and their two adopted children who she describes as 'smashing kids'. She works in her local bookshop and as a Home Tutor for Stockport Education Department, working intensively with children who are not attending school. Her particular interest is pupils who suffer from school phobia.

Frances began writing seriously in 1991. She belongs to Marple Writers' Workshop and Manchester Poets and finds other writers a vital support for the loneliness and difficulty of writing poetry.

Sheila Parry
I have been writing poetry for over fifty years and have been fortunate in having some of my work previously published. I write, as someone said, 'not

for my living but for my life', and although many of my poems are personal, they are not all autobiographical.

I trained as a teacher and gained my degree as a mature student. Since taking early retirement I divide my time between giving private tuition, drama workshops, tutoring WEA classes in Writing and Literature, and working for Oxfam.

I have two sons and my proudest achievement is to be Katherine's grandmother.

I am a member of Chester Poets and the Chester Literature Festival Committee and enjoy taking part in public readings in the North West.

Pat Winslow

Pat Winslow is 39 and lives in Bolton. She has had poetry published in *Beyond Paradise* (Crocus 1990) and in the *Chester Poets Anthology*. A short story of hers appears in *Herzone* (Crocus 1991) and another one is due to be published in *Unknown Territory* (Onlywomen Press 1993). She is currently writing a novel.

When she is not writing she runs adult education and community arts courses - anything from creative writing to reminiscence workshops. A former actor, she still finds herself drafted into occasional theatre projects as well.

Pat's ambition is to become more accurate and faithful in her writing. Her other ambition is to be financially solvent one day.

Acknowledgements

The poems below, or earlier versions, have been previously published as indicated.

Frances Nagle
Purveyors - *Outposts* (Hippopotamus Press 1993)
Visit to the Illuminator - *Network Northwest* (BBC Radio)
Looking for Heathcliff - *Network Northwest* (BBC Radio)
Some of these poems have appeared in - *Envoi, Envoi Summer Anthology 1991, Poetry Nottingham, The Rialto, Staple.*

Sheila Parry
Hostage - *Chester Poets 17, IMP Magazine* (September 1992)
Young Love - *Chester Poets 14*
Easter Flowers - *Chester Poets 16*
The Literary Circus - *IMP Magazine* (September 1992)
Untouchables - *Chester Poets 17*
The Lines are Down (To D.C.) - *Chester Poets 16*
Summer Wedding - *Chester Poets 17*
Table Talk - *Poetry Digest 1988*
Return Visit - *Chester Poets 16*
Exchanging Gifts - *New Prospect 1990*

Pat Winslow
Ivory - *Co-op Caring Poetry Festival* (1992)
Barry Manilow - *Chester Poets 17*
Two Moons - September 16th 1992 - *Never Bury Poetry, winter 16* (1992)

About Commonword

Commonword is a not-for-profit community publishing co-operative, producing books by writers in the North West, and supporting and developing their work. In this way Commonword brings new writing to a wide audience.

Over a period of sixteen years Commonword has published poetry, short stories and other forms of creative writing. *Five Women Poets* is the fifteenth title to be published under the Crocus imprint.

In general, Commonword seeks to encourage the creative writing and publishing of the diverse groups in society who have lacked, or been excluded from, the means of expression through the written word. Working-class writers, Black people, women, disabled people, lesbians and gay men all too often fall into this category.

To give writers the opportunity to develop their work in an informal setting, Commonword offers a variety of writers' workshops, such as Womanswrite, the Monday Night Group and Northern Gay Writers.

... and Cultureword

Cultureword, a part of Commonword which acts as a focus for Asian, Chinese and African-Caribbean writers, organises Black writers' workshops, poetry performances and training events.

Through Commonword's Writers Agency we can also arrange for writers to perform their work or facilitate creative writing workshops in schools or other settings.

In addition to writers' workshops and publishing, Commonword offers a manuscript reading service to give constructive criticism, and can give information and advice to writers about facilities in their immediate locality.

The Commonword/Cultureword offices are at Cheetwood House, 21 Newton street, Manchester M1 1FZ. Our phone number is (061) 236 2773. We would like to hear from you.

Recent Crocus titles

Dancing on Diamonds
Poetry and short stories from thirty-six young writers. Lively and provocative.
'The past revisited, the future seen with hopeful vision and the anger of the innocent. A collection of contemporary thoughts by a new breed of contemporary writers - a real pleasure.' (Art Malik)
ISBN 0 946745 06 4
Price £5.95 Pbk

The Delicious Lie
This book marks the arrival of a fresh, highly talented new voice onto the British poetry scene.
'What a wonderful, wonderful slice of love and life this is. A gorgeous, scrumptious piece of poetic justice from new(ish) writer Georgina Blake.' (Nayaba Aghedo, City Life)
'Georgina Blake is a very talented poet. Her work is illuminated by a fine intelligence, a clever wit and a warm heart. The poems in The Delicious Lie gave me great pleasure. She writes so eloquently about the feelings we all have but cannot articulate. Georgina deserves to be read by a huge audience.' (Sue Townsend)
ISBN 0 946745 07 2
Price £4.95 Pbk

Rainbows In The Ice
This book of poetry demonstrates the wealth of creative talent that exists within the disabled community. A unique and memorable collection.
'An impressive anthology ... It's good to read poets who remember that expressing and eliciting

emotion are the centrepieces of writing effective poetry.' (Robert Hamberger, Mailout)
'A lovely collection of poetry by some highly talented people.' (Jackie Glatter, Mencap News)
ISBN 0 946745 90 0
Price £4.50 Pbk

A Matter of Fat

This incisive and humorous novel follows the fortunes of Stella, the leader of 'Slim-Plicity', a commercial slimming club, and some of the club members. When a Fat Women's Support Group starts up nearby, complications soon follow ...
'In A Matter of Fat, Ashworth has retained a wicked sense of humour, while raising some very important questions.' (New Woman)
'Sherry Ashworth writes with wit, compassion, excruciating honesty, and controlled, creative anger.' (Zoe Fairbairns, Everywoman)
ISBN 0 946745 95 1
Price £4.95 Pbk

Flame

A dual language book of poetry in English and Urdu by Asian writers. Love, home life, racism and other political issues are some of the areas explored by the fifteen talented poets in Flame. Translations are by Alishan Zaidi.
'One of the best collections of Asian poetry I have read.' (Kam Kaur, Eastern Eye)
'Powerful and distinctive ... a pleasure to read.' (Shelley Khair, Yorkshire Artscene)
ISBN 0 946745 85 4
Price £4.50 Pbk

Herzone

Fantasy short stories by women. Ranging from science fiction, to 'twist in the tale' stories and mythical fantasies, this collection has something to delight and entertain everyone.

'There is nothing but pleasure to be gained from these tales.' (Manchester Evening News)

'A varied and satisfying collection.' (Zoe Fairbairns, Everywoman)

ISBN 0 946745 80 3

Price £4.50 Pbk

Beyond Paradise

An original collection of poetry that celebrates the vitality of gay and lesbian writing. Provocative, funny and touching, Beyond Paradise offers fresh perspectives on life in the '90s - and beyond!

'I promise you, once you've read it, you'll keep coming back for another little glimpse of life in the lesbian and gay lane.' (Scene Out)

'The tragic nature of human existence, the fun and joy of being alive are here ...' (Gay Times)

ISBN 0 946745 75 7

Price £4.50 Pbk

Relative to Me ...

Short stories on family life. Families can be a source of inspiration - or desperation! The stories in Relative to Me ... show both, with a wonderful mix of serious and light-hearted writing.

'Relative to Me ... proves there's plenty of talent just waiting to burst forth from the region.' (Manchester Metro News)

'Twenty refreshingly original tales.' (The Teacher)

ISBN 0 946745 70 6

Price £3.95 Pbk

Talkers Through Dream Doors
Fourteen talented Black women write about their
lives in this collection of poetry and short stories.
ISBN 0 946745 60 9
Price £3.50 Pbk

Now Then
Poetry and short stories illustrating lifestyles,
work and leisure from 1945 to the present day.
ISBN 0 946745 55 2
Price £3.50 PBK

Holding Out
Women's lives are portrayed with realism,
frankness and fun in this excellent collection of
twenty-one short stories.
ISBN 0 946745 30 7
Price £3.50 Pbk

Other titles from Commonword
Black and Priceless, poetry and short stories.
0 946745 45 5, £3.50
Between Mondays, poetry from the Monday Night
Group. 0 946745 35 8, £2.50
Identity magazine, poetry and articles by Asian
and African- Caribbean writers. £0.95
Liberation Soldier, poetry by Joe Smythe.
0 946745 25 0, £2.50
Poetic Licence, poetry from Greater Manchester.
0 946745 40 4, £2.50
Turning Points, a Northern Gay Writers collection.
0 946745 20 X, £2.95

For a recent catalogue of all our titles, write to:
Crocus books/Commonword
Cheetwood House
21 Newton Street
Manchester M1 1FZ

**If you are visually impaired and would
like this book, or any of our other titles, to
be produced on audio-tape please contact
us.**

ORDER FORM

TITLE	QUANTITY	PRICE
Dancing on Diamonds		£5.95
The Delicious Lie		£4.95
Rainbows In The Ice		£4.50
A Matter of Fat		£4.95
Herzone		£4.50
Flame		£4.50
Beyond Paradise		£4.50
Relative To Me ...		£3.95
Talkers Through Dream Doors		£3.50
Black and Priceless		£3.50
Holding Out		£3.50
Identity magazine		£0.95
Poetic Licence		£2.50
Liberation Soldier		£2.50
Turning Points		£2.95

TOTAL

Please send a cheque or postal order, made payable to
Commonword Ltd, covering the purchase price plus 50p
per book for postage and packing.

NAME ....

ADDRESS ....

.... POSTCODE ....

Please return to: Commonword, Cheetwood House, 21
Newton Street, Manchester M1 1 FZ.